TITANIC

IN PICTURES

Contents

4

8

44

22

Introduction	4
White Star Line and the Birth of the *Titanic*	8
The Interior	22
The Passengers	26
The Crew	38
The Disaster	44
Following the Disaster	52
Remembering the *Titanic*	62

52

First published in the UK in 2011 by Instinctive Product Development

© Instinctive Product Development 2012

www.instinctivepd.com

Printed in China

ISBN: 978-1-907657-71-9

Designed by: BrainWave

Creative Director: Kevin Gardner

Written by: Henry Hirst

Images courtesy of Shutterstock, Mirrorpix and Creative Commons

Introduction

April 2012 will see the incredible milestone of 100 years since the terrible tragedy that befell the RMS *Titanic*. It seems incredible that 100 years after its launch the story of the *Titanic* still fascinates us as deep under the ocean her remains are rapidly rotting and decaying.

Following the death of Millvina Dean in 2009, the last survivor of the sinking of the *Titanic* who was rescued as a baby as the liner sank, the last living link with one of the most significant maritime tragedies in history has disappeared.

Although too young to remember the actual event, her presence ensured that there remained a tangible connection to the sinking. Almost a century after the actual loss of the supposedly unsinkable White Star Line vessel, interest in the history of the ship, its passengers and crew, and with its ill-fated maiden voyage remains intense.

In some respects the fascination with the *Titanic* seems to not take into account its relative place in history. It wasn't the worst maritime loss of life that had ever taken place and, wasn't the first disaster to have afflicted White Star Line during its relatively short and eventful life.

The romance of a ship that failed to complete a single voyage, lost under the waves for three generations until the discovery of the wreck by Robert Ballard and his team, seems to still have resonance today 100 years on. The compelling stories of the heroic struggle amongst many of those involved in the sinking to help others, the sacrifice made by many of the passengers and crew and the behaviour of those that were only interested in protecting themselves all continue to both inspire and appal us.

Whether rich or poor, first-, second- or third-class passengers, the ocean did not care, those that died and those that were saved included all – the tragedy of those travelling to America in search of a new and better life only to die on board the 'unsinkable ship' alongside some of the richest of society.

The story of the *Titanic* will continue to be told over the coming years alongside precious photos and memorabilia that remind us of the human tragedy.

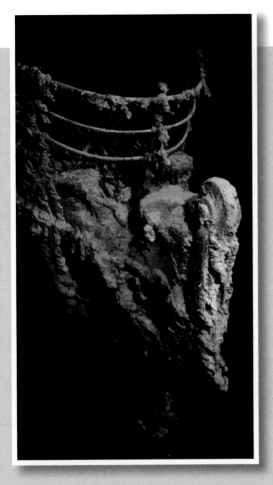

- **ABOVE:** The romance of the *Titanic*.
- **LEFT:** Robert Ballard's discovery of the *Titanic*.
- **OPPOSITE INSET:** Millvina Dean pictured in 1999.
- **BELOW:** The *Titanic* prior to her maiden voyage.

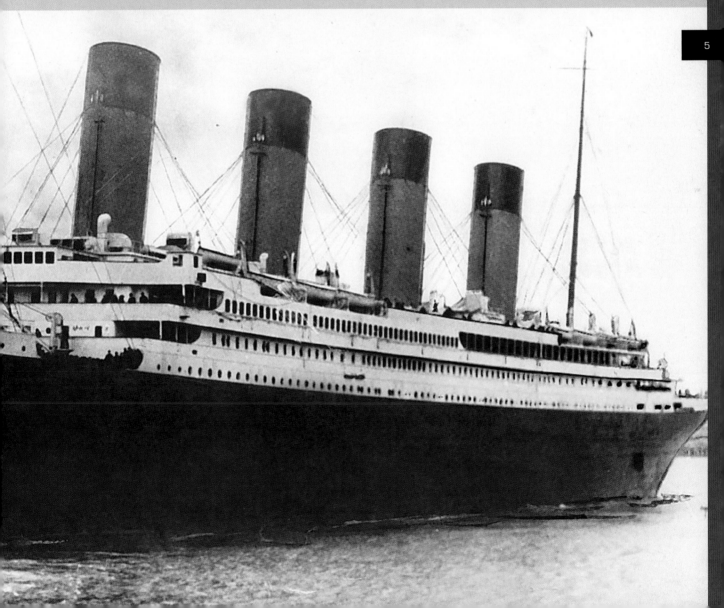

R·M·S TITANIC ·
TITANIC
COPYRIGHT.
THE WESTER
25,000 OFFICES
This Company TRANSMITS and DELIVERS
THEO. N. VAIL, PRESIDENT
RECEIVED AT

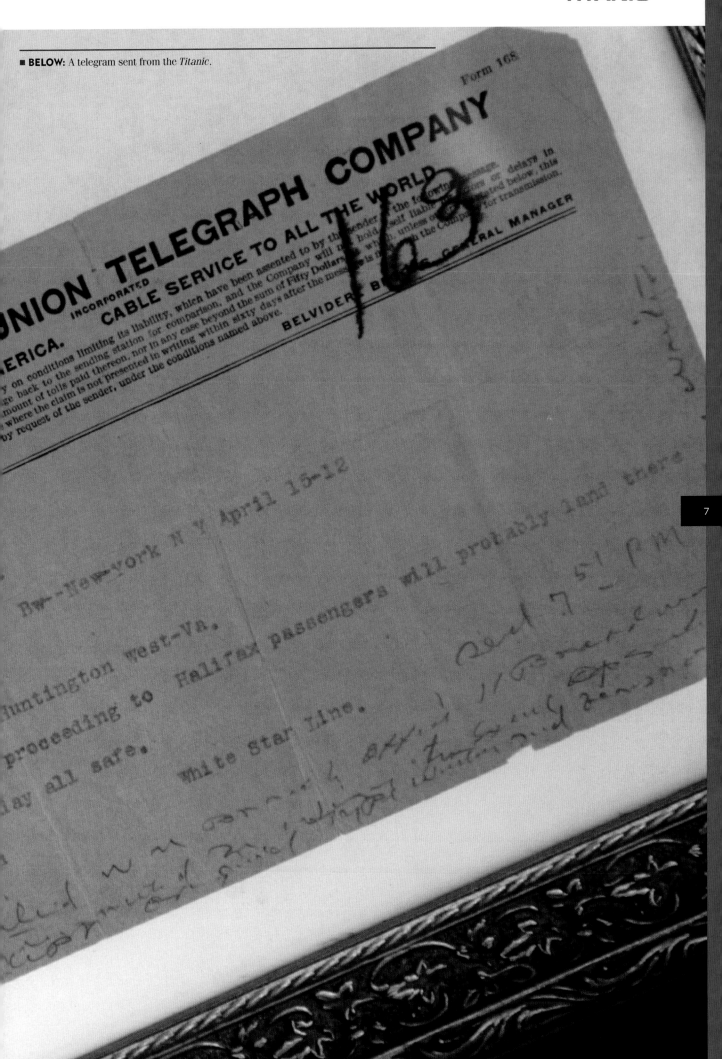

■ **BELOW:** A telegram sent from the *Titanic*.

White Star Line and the Birth of the *Titanic*

Although the shipping line that was ultimately to become the White Star Line had its origins earlier in the 19ᵗʰ century, when it concentrated on traffic to and from Australia, the history of the company that will forever be associated with the *Titanic* can be said to date from January 1868 when Thomas Ismay, father of Joseph Bruce Ismay, (the chairman and managing director of International Mercantile Marine in April 1912), bought the assets of the bankrupt White Star Line for £1,000.

■ **BELOW:** The *Titanic* in the background at the Harland and Wolff shipyard in Belfast.

Ismay took the decision to change the core operations of the company into a business more focused on the transatlantic trade. This was to capitalise on the countless thousands who were making their way to North America trying to escape the poverty of Europe for the wealth that the New World seemed to offer.

New finance was needed for the business, which was to be based in Liverpool, and Ismay was able to secure the backing of German financier Gustav Schwabe. Schwabe had already become involved in the Belfast shipyard of Harland & Wolff and he was prepared to back the new business with the provision that White Star Line acquired all its new ships from Harland & Wolff.

White Star and Harland & Wolff were to have a long relationship, from the first ship to be completed – the *Oceanic* launched in August 1870 – right the way to the three great liners – the *Olympic*, *Titanic* and the *Britannic*. These historic ships were all constructed between 1908 and 1915.

White Star Line was not vested with much good luck and fortune with a high accident ratio and on 20 March 1873, the company's second steamship – the *Atlantic* – set sail from Liverpool on her 19th crossing of the Atlantic. As there was not enough coal on board the ship was

■ **TOP:** Thomas Ismay, chairman of International Mercantile & Marine.

■ **ABOVE:** Bruce Ismay.

■ **ABOVE:** John Pierpont Morgan who was booked on the *Titanic* but cancelled.

■ **ABOVE LEFT:** RMS *Oceanic*.

■ **LEFT:** The Steamship *Atlantic* foundered on rocks off Meagher's Island, Newfoundland, April 1873.

■ **BELOW:** The third great liner *Britannic*.

forced to divert to Halifax, Nova Scotia, and got into difficulties just off Meagher's Island, Newfoundland on the morning of 1 April 1873. As with the *Titanic*, the *Atlantic* was not provided with a suitable number of lifeboats for the passengers and crew and 565 of the 966 on board died in the disaster.

Despite proposals to merge with Cunard later in the decade, White Star managed to retain its independence until the early part of the 20th century when John Pierpont Morgan, who was actually booked on the *Titanic*'s maiden voyage but later cancelled, tried to create a monopoly of shipping on the North Atlantic route in order to raise prices and increase profitability. Through his International Mercantile Marine Company, Morgan acquired a number of British shipping lines – including White Star in February 1904 . His approach to acquire the British-owned Cunard line failed when the British government gave Cunard a loan to construct the *Lusitania* and *Mauretania*, along with a lucrative contract for carrying mail.

It was the development of the two Cunard liners that provided the ambition to build three 'Olympic' type ships for White Star. Designed by a number of Harland & Wolff officials, including Thomas Andrews who would later die when the *Titanic* sank, the ships were not designed for speed – unlike the Cunard vessels – but for luxury, particularly for first- and second-class passengers. The first of the three vessels – the *Olympic* – was laid down in December 1908; the *Olympic* was launched on 20 October 1910

■ **ABOVE:** Thomas Andrews of Harland & Wolff with his family.

■ **LEFT:** All White Star Line ships went through rigorous sea trials before arriving at Southampton docks.

and completed its maiden voyage under the command of White Star Line's commodore, Captain Edward Smith, who was to later captain of the *Titanic*, in June 1911.

The *Olympic* had the misfortune to have two accidents. Although both fairly minor they were significant and perhaps a stark warning of events to come. The first of these took place towards the end of the maiden voyage, on 21 June 1911 when as the ship approached New York, one of the tugs helping to steer the liner to its berth was temporarily crushed under the massive liner's stern. On 20 September 1911, the *Olympic* was hit by the elderly Royal Navy cruiser

■ **ABOVE LEFT:** The *Olympic* after its collision with HMS *Hawke*.

■ **LEFT:** HMS *Hawke* sustained much damage too.

HMS *Hawke* in the Solent at the start of what should have been the liner's fifth crossing of the Atlantic. There was extensive damage to the liner that reached below the water line and concerns over the harmful effects of the collision led to it being sent back to Belfast for a full review of its state. Repairs completed, the *Olympic* departed from Belfast on 20 November 1911. This would not

■ **ABOVE:** *Titanic* & *Olympic* under construction.

■ **RIGHT:** *Titanic* nears completion in the dry dock.

be the only time that *Olympic* would have to return to Belfast before the *Titanic* – laid down on 31 March 1909 – was completed; the loss of a propeller meant a further repair in March 1912. Although the *Olympic* was actually at sea when the *Titanic* sank, the ship was too far away to offer assistance to the stricken ship.

The *Titanic* was just six inches longer than its sister ship *Olympic*

with a tonnage of 46,238. Its vast size included the well recognised four funnel system and it was fitted with 16 supposedly watertight compartments designed to close one-by-one if required should there be any danger spotted by those on the bridge. However despite this attempt to create an 'unsinkable' ship, this was later proven to be a major factor in the sinking of the *Titanic* as water was able to reach over the compartment into the next and so on. The *Titanic* reached its launch date of 31 May 1911; such was the interest in the ship that tens of thousands of people attended along with many other dignitaries

and people associated with the White Star Line. It was a proud day for all concerned with the construction of the ship.

Various delays contributed to *Titanic* being unable to start her sea trials until early April in 1912. Captain Edward Smith was taking charge of the *Titanic* for the first time not knowing of the fate his new, beautiful liner faced. Along with Smith were the various staff and crew who were operating the giant liner for its sea trials and a proud Thomas Andrews of Harland & Wolff was also on board.

The sea trials only took place for one day with pressure upon those

■ **ABOVE:** One of the mechanical bulkhead doors.

■ **OPPOSITE LEFT:** *Titanic* rudder before launch.

■ **LEFT:** *Titanic* leaves the dry dock in Belfast.

WHITE STAR LINE.

"OLYMPIC." 45,000 TONS. AND "TITANIC." 45,000 TONS.

THE LARGEST STEAMERS IN THE WORLD.

ALL STEAMERS BUILT IN IRELAND.

QUEENSTOWN-NEW YORK
ON THURSDAYS AND FRIDAYS.

QUEENSTOWN-BOSTON
ON WEDNESDAYS.

For Freight and Passage apply to

JOHN DENNEHY,
Insurance Agent, CAHIRCIVEEN, Co. Kerry.

taking part to ensure *Titanic* was given the all clear. The ship received its Board of Trade certificate and was handed over officially to White Star Line. The liner then headed south to Southampton for the start of its ill-fated maiden voyage.

Following the loss of the *Titanic* modifications were made to the *Olympic*, most notably in the increased provision of lifeboats, and to the *Britannic* then under construction (having been laid down on 30 November 1911). Both the remaining two liners were to serve the military during World War 1. The *Olympic* survived this period and

was returned to passenger service at the end of hostilities; the *Britannic*, however, was to be less fortunate. Never actually entering passenger service, the ship was requisitioned as a hospital ship following completion of sea trials in May 1915. *Britannic* was to sink as a result of hitting a mine en route to Gallipoli on 21 May 1916. Although the ship's bulkheads had been modified in the light of the loss of the *Titanic*, such was the damage that the ship was to sink albeit with the loss of only 30 lives. The only surviving member of the trio – the *Olympic* – soldiered on to the 1930s and the liner was to be

■ **ABOVE:** *Titanic* and SS *New York* almost collide.
■ **OPPOSITE LEFT:** White Star Line poster of RMS *Titanic*.
■ **BELOW:** *Titanic* tickets, first, second and third class.

taken out of service in 1935 following the merger of White Star Line and Cunard, being initially cannibalised at Jarrow on the Tyne, with fixtures and fittings auctioned off, before the hulk was scrapped at Inverkeithing in Scotland. The scrapping of the *Olympic* was completed in 1937.

After the *Titanic* disaster, White Star Line continued to operate until the late 1920s when the economic conditions, particularly after the Wall Street Crash of 1929, deteriorated. Brokered by the British government, the old rivals Cunard and White Star merged in May 1934. The new company – Cunard-White Star Ltd – was partially owned by the shareholders of Cunard and gradually the larger company came to dominate. In 1947, shareholders of the erstwhile White Star Line were bought out and the company reverted to being Cunard alone.

■ **RIGHT:** RMS *Olympic* postcard.

■ **ABOVE:** *Britannic* being used in World War 1 as a hospital ship.

■ **BELOW:** *Olympic* leaves for Inverkeithing in Scotland, to be broken up.

The Interior

Unlike the new liners built for Cunard, which were unashamedly designed for speed and competing in the Blue Riband for the fastest crossing of the Atlantic, the *Titanic* and the other two White Star ships were conceived to be amongst the most luxurious ever constructed – and this luxury, unusually, extended even to the relative facilities offered to third-class passengers. It was widely considered that the third-class accommodation and common rooms were as luxurious as second-class accommodation on many other contemporary liners.

There were three main components that made up the interior of the ship: the passenger accommodation, the crew accommodation and the space required to make the vessel function. There were seven main passenger decks – A to G – with the Boat Deck located above Deck A and with the Orlop Deck and the Tank Top below Deck G. All decks below Deck D were split partially or completely by the casings for the boiler rooms and for the engine room.

There were 25 huge boilers which were distributed throughout the ship in six separate boiler rooms – ranging from No 6 towards the bow of the liner to No 1 located amidships. In order to fire the furnaces the *Titanic* set sail from Southampton with some 5,900 tons of coal on board; experience with the *Olympic* suggested that the ship would use some 600 tons of coal per day.

■ **ABOVE:** The magnificence of the grand staircase.

■ **ABOVE RIGHT:** One of the *Titanic* boat decks.

■ **RIGHT:** Replica *Titanic* Grand Staircase.

■ **ABOVE:** Junior radio operator Harold Bride.

■ **LEFT:** *Titanic's* boiler room.

■ **ABOVE:** *Titanic's* luxurious interior.

The coal was stored around the furnaces and reserve coal bunkers.

Aft of Boiler Room No 1 was the engine room; this accommodated two huge reciprocating four-cylinder, triple expansion steam engines, to power the side propellers, and behind these was a single low-press Parsons steam turbine, which powered the central propeller. These three engines were designed to provide all the power needed to move the vessel through the water. Further back were sited four steam-powered electrical generators; these provided all the electricity required for use on board. Amongst features incorporated on

board the liner that required power were three lifts – two of which were for the exclusive use of first-class passengers and the third for second class – electric lighting throughout and the Marconi radio room. The ship was not, however, fitted with a public address system. The radio room was located on the port side of the Boat Deck; it was from here that passengers could send and receive messages for a fee. As part of the commercial arrangement that allowed Marconi to base staff on board ships like the *Titanic*, free transmission of messages between officers and company and inter-ship

was permitted. The radios, rated at 1.56kW, had a range of some 400 miles and operators could hear the transmissions made to and from other ships within range; this was to be of significance as the tragedy gradually unfolded.

Also situated on the Boat Deck was the bridge, the wheelhouse, the cabins occupied by the senior officers – known as the 'Officers' House' – and the gymnasium. This, like a number of other facilities, was for the exclusive use of first-class passengers. Located on Deck F – known as the Middle Deck – were the swimming pool, the squash court and the

Turkish bath. All of these were again for the exclusive use of first-class passengers. The swimming pool was sited on the starboard side; this was filled with salt water to a depth of six feet and was also provided with two showers and changing cubicles. Male passengers could use the pool free of charge between 6am and 9am; thereafter there was a fee payable of $1 or four-shillings. Women had exclusive use between 10am and 1pm and men again from 2pm to 6pm. The squash court was located forward of the swimming pool; again a fee was payable. The Turkish bath was located on the port side and was used exclusively by women between 10am and 1pm and by men between 2pm and 6pm.

The Promenade Deck (A) accommodated the first-class lounge, reading and writing room, smoke room and verandas as well as a number of the smaller first-class cabins. The first-class lounge was fitted out with wooden panelling, carvings lit by candelabra and huge mirrors; it was a room that could have graced one of the world's most luxurious hotels. The smoking room was panelled in mahogany inlaid with mother-of-pearl and was provided with ornate framed screens of stained glass.

■ **BELOW:** The luxurious gymnasium.

Below Deck A came the Bridge Deck (B); on this level was situated the second-class smoke room, the à la carte restaurant and the Café Parisien – the latter being an addition to the design from that of the earlier *Olympic* – along with a number of first-class cabins and suites. The luxurious restaurant was available to both first- and second-class passengers which was open throughout the day and was run by Luigi Gatti who had recruited staff from some of his London restaurants to work in the ship's restaurant. The restaurant could sit up to 137 passengers at any one time.

The next deck down was the Shelter Deck (C) which provided the library, lavishly decorated with stunning tapestries and silk drapes, along with the third-class general and smoking rooms. There were further first-class cabins on this deck.

Saloon Deck (D) also held the last of the first-class accommodation along with the second-class dining area which held almost 400 people along with the first-class dining room which held an even larger 532 people when fully occupied. Like other public areas these were lavishly decorated rooms. Forward

■ **ABOVE:** The third-class quarters.

of the first-class dining saloon was the first-class reception room; this and the impressive staircase leading up from it to the decks above were amongst the most sumptuous of the public spaces on board the *Titanic*. Like all the public areas the staircase was a stunning and eye-catching centrepiece. Towards the stern of this deck was second- and third-class accommodation.

Further second- and third-class accommodation was provided on the Upper Deck (E) and the Middle Deck (F); the third-class dining saloons were also located on Deck F. The final passenger accommodation – again third class – was to be found on the Lower Deck (G).

25

The Passengers

The *Titanic* was built to carry a staggering 3,547 passengers of which the staff and crew accounted for 944. The loss of life would have been much higher if *Titanic* had been full to its capacity but on that fateful voyage there were a total of 2,208 passengers and crew. The majority of passengers had boarded at Southampton although a small number were also to board at Cherbourg and at Queenstown; a handful of passengers disembarked at Queenstown as well, most notably Francis M. Browne, a second-class passenger and later Catholic priest, whose photographs of the doomed liner's journey from Southampton to Queenstown form a priceless record of the ship prior to its loss.

■ **BELOW:** The second-class promenade deck on the ill-fated White Star Line liner.

■ **FAR LEFT:** A photo taken by Francis M. Browne of *Titanic*.

■ **LEFT:** John and Madeleine Astor.

PASSENGERS BOARDING THE TITANIC AT QUEENSTOWN AND SOME OF THE VICTIMS AND SURVIVORS OF HISTORY'S MOST TERRIBLE SHIPWRECK.

Chief Purser McElroy (clean-shaven) and Dr. W. F. N. O'Loughlin, the chief ship's surgeon. Both are missing.

Mr. K. H. Behr, the famous tennis player, saved.

Sir Cosmo Duff-Gordon, Bart., and his wife, who is better known as "Lucile." Both of them are reported saved.

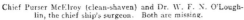
Embarking on the Titanic at Queenstown last Thursday. This was the last port at which the ill-starred vessel called.

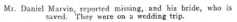
Mr. Daniel Marvin, reported missing, and his bride, who is saved. They were on a wedding trip.

Mr. Head (missing), a prominent member of Lloyd's.

Colonel J. J. and Mrs. Astor, returning from their honeymoon. She is saved, but his body has been picked up dead.

Of the third-class passengers relatively little is known about them individually; the vast majority were migrants from Scandinavia and Europe seeking a better life in the New World. Although facilities on the *Titanic* were better than most for these travellers, their accommodation was on the lower decks and so third-class passengers were more vulnerable when the ship foundered than those travelling first or second class. Moreover, during the actual evacuation of the stricken ship, it seems that some of these passengers were discouraged from boarding the lifeboats by the crew in favour of those from first and second class.

In terms of the fascination with the *Titanic*, it is many of the passengers in first and second class that inevitably grab the attention, including as it did some of the wealthiest names in society at the time.

The wealthiest man on board the *Titanic* was John Jacob Astor IV. Born

■ **ABOVE:** Some of the victims and survivors of the *Titanic*.

■ **OPPOSITE RIGHT:** The true love story of the *Titanic*.

■ **OPPOSITE BELOW:** More notable passengers including Benjamin Guggenheim.

in 1864, his family had vast trading interests in the fur trade, property and hotels. Astor's presence on the *Titanic* was due to the fact that, in 1911, he had married 18-year-old Madeleine Talmadge Force and, in order to allow the scandal

Titanic lovers who inspired *that* film

REAL-LIFE ROMANCE REVEALED FOR FIRST TIME

Daily Mirror
WEDNESDAY 20.08.2008 M 25

RICHARD SMITH
richard.smith@mirror.co.uk

IT was one of the biggest blockbusters in movie history – shooting Kate Winslet and Leonardo Di Caprio to international stardom.

But the real-life romance that was the inspiration for their heart-rending scenes in the film Titanic was revealed yesterday by one of the survivors' descendants.

Joanna Wood, 47, says the love story was based on her great-aunt Roberta Maioni, a maid travelling first class on the Titanic's doomed maiden voyage in 1912.

She met and instantly fell in love with a young ship's steward, who died as the ship sank – after giving her his life jacket and helping her into a lifeboat.

As a final gesture, he pressed his official White Star liner badge into her hand, leaving her with a final poignant memento.

Roberta and her employer, Countess Lucy Rothes, were among those rescued by the Carpathia and travelled on to New York.

But she never forgot her short-lived romance aboard the Titanic or the terrible night when more than 1,500 passengers and crew died.

Roberta wrote a poem describing her feelings, as well as a seven-page account of the horrors she witnessed.

The poem, her writings, the badge and a photograph of Roberta fetched £10,000 when they went under the hammer at a little-publicised auction in 1999.

Joanna, from Totnes, Devon, only revealed the true amazing story

MAID IN HEAVEN Family snap of Roberta as a young woman

▲ **CLASSIC** Kate and Leonardo in film

when she attended a Titanic exhibition at Torquay museum describing her relative's ordeal and what happened to her other heirlooms.

She said: "This story is part of our family history. The crew member who gave the White Star badge to Roberta also gave her his life jacket and put her in the lifeboat.

"There's a direct link between Roberta's story and the movie.

"I think they used it as the inspiration for the love story."

Roberta died in 1963 aged 71. She married in 1919 but had no children.

Joanna said: "When I was young I used to wear these taffeta dresses and I wore them again and again.

"They were Roberta's but I didn't know it at the time. I wore them out. They were unique but I only learned that they were hers four years later. I'm sorry I didn't look after them."

"Also there was a locket, which was gold, with blue enamel and a pearl and it belonged to Roberta.

"I think someone took the handbag it was in and I couldn't believe it when I saw it on TV show Flog It, which was filmed in Torquay.

"If I knew who bought it I would want to buy it back. It's priceless to me because of its sentimental value.

"The person who bought it won't know about its origins.

"If they did they'd know it was worth a few bob."

2,220 PEOPLE ON BOARD TITANIC WHEN IT SANK IN 1912. JUST 700 WERE SAVED.

▼ **VOYAGE TO HELL** Her first class ticket to journey on the ill-fated liner

▼ **SURVIVOR** Roberta and the badge her lover gave her as a farewell gift

▼ **POEM** Roberta recounts her ordeal on note paper at New York hotel

---

 Mr. Benj. Guggenheim.

 Miss Gladys Cherry.

Major A. Peuchen.

 Miss Esther Bowen.

 Mr. W. T. Stead.

■ **ABOVE:** Isidor Straus, owner of Macy's store, perished along with his wife Ida who refused her place on a lifeboat to stay with her husband.

■ **RIGHT:** The Unsinkable Molly Brown.

to die down – he was after all 47 at the time and his new wife was younger than his son – the newly-weds travelled to Europe. During these travels, the new Mrs Astor had become pregnant and, desirous of having the new child born in the USA, Astor and his party booked a passage on the *Titanic* and were amongst those that boarded during the ship's brief stop at Cherbourg. As was very well reported following the disaster John Jacob Astor IV had told the crew manning the lifeboats that his wife was expecting thus ensuring a place on a boat for her and he also aided Molly Brown in securing her place but was himself to perish.

Another scion of a wealthy US family to be booked on board the *Titanic* was Benjamin Guggenheim, born in 1865, who was travelling back to the USA with his mistress. Like the Astors, the Guggenheim party boarded the ill-fated ship during its call at Cherbourg.

Guggenheim's quote after his female travelling companions had boarded the lifeboat of 'We've dressed up in our best and are prepared to go down like gentlemen' became one of the most remembered with Guggenheim himself perishing

as the boat sunk into the cold waters surrounding the ship.

Many passengers refused to get onto lifeboats, instead remaining with loved-ones and partners preferring to face death rather than save themselves by boarding

■ **TOP & ABOVE:** Lady Duff-Gordon and the Duff-Gordons after being rescued by the *Carpathia*.

the lifeboats on their own. This was much repeated throughout that horrific night and the terrible screams that must have been heard by those escaping to safety would have echoed in the night leaving horrendous memories despite the elation of escape.

Much has been made of some of the more famous, rich and notorious survivors of the *Titanic* disaster including 'The Unsinkable Molly Brown'. Some of these escapes were reviewed at the inquiry into the tragedy including that of Sir Cosmo Edmund Duff-Gordon who had apparently reached safety via a lifeboat that held only 12 people although it should have held many more. Considering the lack of lifeboat provision on the *Titanic* was a major

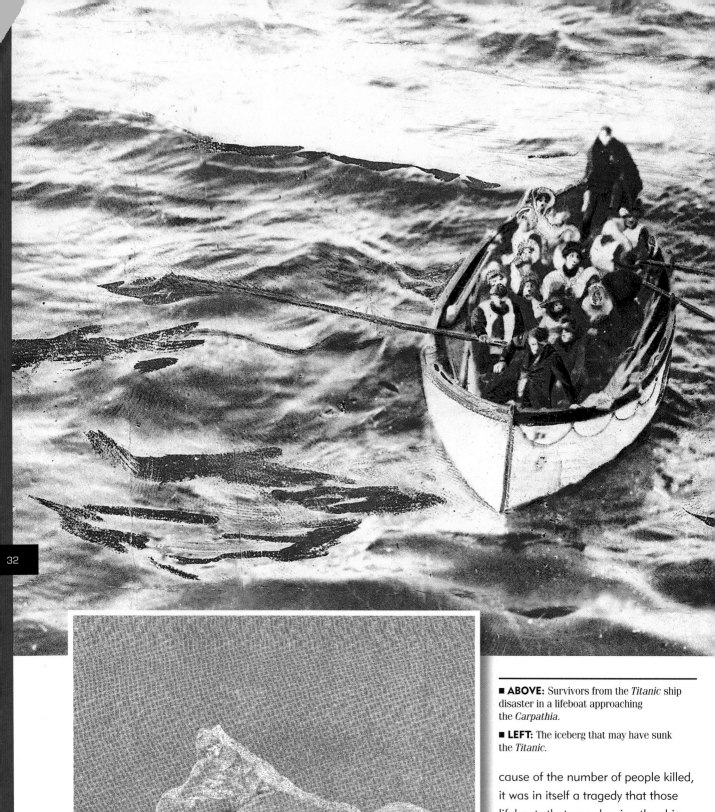

■ **ABOVE:** Survivors from the *Titanic* ship disaster in a lifeboat approaching the *Carpathia*.

■ **LEFT:** The iceberg that may have sunk the *Titanic*.

cause of the number of people killed, it was in itself a tragedy that those lifeboats that were leaving the ship were in many cases not even close to being full to capacity. Duff-Gordon's escape was fortuitous rather than due to any other factors – other than incompetence and a lack of organisation – of the evacuation of the ship. He had in fact boarded the lifeboat having asked if he could get on, permission to do so was granted despite the fact that women and children should have been evacuated as a priority. Clearly such was the

■ **TOP:** An upturned lifeboat found after the disaster.

■ **RIGHT:** Lawrence Beesley (right) pictured in the gymnasium of the *Titanic*.

high emotion of both passengers and crew that any attempts to leave for safety would be taken.

Duff-Gordon was not the only male passenger to escape in this manner with schoolteacher Lawrence Beesley also leaving the *Titanic* in such a way and he later wrote a book on the tragedy, which is still available today. It presents a fascinating account of what happened.

Many other people were sure to drown once the ship started its certain descent to the bottom of the ocean. Some of them were thrown

■ **ABOVE:** Painting depicting the sinking of the *Titanic*.

from the ship due to the velocity of the water flowing through the vessel. Many of these were dragged down with the ship, itself a horrific and dreadful way to die, but some were luckier and were able to swim to a lifeboat where they were dragged on board by other survivors.

Surprising to the vast majority of people at the time was the survival of Joseph Bruce Ismay who was managing director of International Mercantile Marine. He was found on board the *Carpathia* following the recovery of some of the lifeboats and his survival was the subject of much derision in the newspapers at the time who felt that he had boarded the lifeboat at the expense of a woman or child although he vehemently denied that this was the case.

Thomas Andrews, who had earlier inspected the damage with Captain Edward Smith, was one of the true heroes on board; having realised that the boat was going to sink he had ensured that many passengers reached lifeboats and himself died as the ship sank below the waves.

Apart from the three classes of

■ **ABOVE:** Bruce Ismay (right), one of the survivors of the *Titanic*.

■ **RIGHT:** Thomas Andrews.

passenger, there were a number of other travellers on board the *Titanic* who were neither passengers nor employees of the White Star Line. Of these the most prominent were the radio operators – Harold Bride, who was to survive the disaster, and John Phillips, known as 'Jack' who was to lose his life – who were employed, as was common practice at the time, by the Marconi International Marine Communications Co Ltd.

The *Titanic* was a designated Royal Mail Ship (RMS) and part of her planned role was to ship mail to and from North America and there were, therefore, five postal clerks – three American and two British – on board, whose task it was to sort the mail prior to arrival in the sorting room on the starboard side of Deck G. These individuals were employed by the postal authorities. Also in the indeterminate area between crew and passenger, there was Gaspare Antonio Pietro Gatti – known as Luigi – who held the franchise for the à la carte first-class restaurant and who employed directly 67 staff, mainly

WHITE STAR
LINE

T. S.S. TITANIC.

THE NEW YORK HERALD.

THE TITANIC SINKS WITH 1,800 ON BOARD; ONLY 675, MOSTLY WOMEN AND CHILDREN, SAVED

MOST APPALLING DISASTER IN MARINE HISTORY OCCURS WHEN WORLD'S LARGEST STEAMSHIP STRIKES GIGANTIC ICEBERG AT NIGHT

■ **TOP:** *New York Herald* headline.

■ **ABOVE:** John Phillips, Marconi operator.

■ **LEFT:** White Star Line postcard.

■ **BELOW:** Wallace Hartley.

DISASTER SURVIVORS REACH GLASGOW : WOMAN'S STORY OF COWARDLY FOREIGNERS.

A. W. Clark, a greaser, of Liverpool, saved from both the Empress of Ireland and the Titanic. Despite his experiences he says that he may go to sea again.

Distributing clothes to the survivors on the Corsican's arrival in port.

Measuring a survivor for new clothes on board the steamer.

Mrs. Kirtley, who, aided by the waterproof coat she was wearing, swam for a mile. To save herself she was compelled to shake off a man who clung to her.

Italian, in the Café Parisien.

One of the most memorable and touching recollections of passengers surviving the disaster was that of the *Titanic* bandleader Wallace Hartley who, with his fellow musicians, was playing music literally 'while the ship sank'. They were determined to try and keep spirits up as clearly most people were terrified and the vision of the band playing on has featured in many films and documentaries that have since covered the disaster.

These were some of the stories that were reported in newspapers of the time where pages and pages were devoted both to the stories of those who perished, particularly the rich and the wealthy, but also to the stories of courage, of those who had to save themselves whilst others less fortunate were to drown.

■ **ABOVE:** Survivors from the *Titanic* reach Glasgow.

■ **RIGHT:** ...And the band played on.

The Crew

At the apex of the ship's crew was the captain. Edward John Smith born in Stoke-on-Trent in 1850, was by far the most experienced captain employed by White Star Line and, as commodore of the line since 1904, one of his privileges was to take command of any new vessel operated by White Star Line on its maiden voyage. On 10 April 1912 he boarded the *Titanic* for the first time in order to command her on the maiden voyage to New York. Captain Smith was ultimately to go down with the ship and his body was never recovered.

Under Smith, there were a number of senior officers. The chief officer was Henry Wilde, a Liverpudlian born in 1872. However, his appointment was made relatively late in the day as, originally, he had been scheduled to sail with the *Olympic* but was transferred to the new ship in early April 1912. Following a career at sea, he had joined White Star Line in July 1897 and had been chief officer on the *Olympic* under Captain Smith from August 1911. Following his appointment, the original second officer – David Blair – did not sail with the ship.

Following the decision to bring Wilde in as chief officer, William Murdoch became the ship's first officer. Born in Scotland in 1873, Murdoch was in command of the liner at the critical point when it struck the iceberg. A career sailor, he had first joined White Star Line in 1900 and had previously been first officer on board the *Olympic* prior to his transfer to the *Titanic* for the new liner's maiden voyage. Murdoch was set to work organising part of the evacuation and perished at sea.

■ **RIGHT:** William Murdoch, Henry Wilde, Joseph Boxhall and Captain Edward John Smith.

■ **BELOW:** Surviving officers: Harold Lowe, Charles Lightoller, Herbert Pitman (sitting) and Joseph Boxhall.

HUNDREDS OF FRIENDS AND RELATIVES ANXIOUSLY WAITING FOR NEWS OF THE FA...

Mr. B. Webb, a smoke-room steward on the ill-fated liner, and his young wife. It is not difficult to imagine the terrible suspense she is enduring.

Mr. W. White, one of the trimmers. He belongs to Southampton.

Mr. G. Kearl, a trimmer. Nothing is yet known of what became of him.

Mr. A. Stanbrook, a fireman. Like most of the crew, his home is at Southampton.

Mr. Sawyer, a window-cleaner, of Southampton. He has four young children.

Mr. F. W. Barrett, a fireman. His fate is still a matter of conjecture.

Mr T. Preston, one of the trimmers, whose fate was uncertain.

Mr. C. J. Joughin, baker, of whom ... anxiously awa...

Miss Stella Sage, one of the family of eleven who are all missing.

Mr. R. Bristow, third-class steward, photographed with his little child.

Mr. Sage, of Peterborough, who, with his wife and nine children, is missing.

This photograph, which has just come to hand, was taken on the Titanic—her deck can just be seen—by a passenger who travelled on her as far as Queenstown. It shows how nearly the ill-starred liner collided with the New York when she left Southampton on her fatal voyage. Alongside the Titanic is the Oceanic.

The Mackay-Bennett, which is steaming towards the scene of the disaster in search of bodies. Coffins are being taken, and several undertakers and embalmers are on board. She also carries a Church of England clergyman.

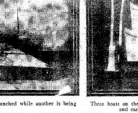
"You're husband is saved," the most welcome news in the world. Mrs. Lightoller is the wife of one of the rescued officers.

Receiving a message yesterday in the Lo... portion of the news concerning the terrib... municate the news

Model of the davits as used on the Titanic. One, two or three boats can be attached to them, but in the case of the wrecked liner there was one boat per davit.

The davits in use. The photograph shows how one boat has been launched while another is being lowered into the water.

Three boats on the davits, and carry between

Mr. T. Hunt, a trimmer. Did he go down with the giant liner?

Mr. S. Williams, a trimmer, whose friends are anxiously awaiting news of him.

Mr. B. Coppenthwaite, one of the firemen. Is he among the saved?

Mr. J. O'Connor, a fireman. Is he among those of the crew who were rescued?

Mr. A. Dore, one of the trimmers. His friends waited for news for 4 days.

Father and son, both of whom were firemen on the Titanic. Both, too, were named A. W. May, strangely en...h.

Mr. W. Taylor, one of the firemen. Nothing is yet known of his fate.

Mr. P. Henry, a fireman. Is he on board the C... Carpathia?

■ **ABOVE:** Awaiting news of the fate of the crew after the disaster.

■ **LEFT:** William Murdoch.

Charles Lightoller was born in 1874 originating from Lancashire. He was on board *Titanic* during its sea trials and was appointed as second officer for its maiden voyage. After aiding with loading some of the lifeboats he was swept overboard and encountered lifeboat B which at the time was itself in a precarious position. He helped to save a number of men who had been capsized by the lifeboat. He survived the tragedy and returned to work for the White Star Line for a brief period afterwards but the effects of the disaster had a huge impact on him personally and on his professional career.

Herbert John Pitman was the *Titanic*'s third officer and he joined White Star in 1906. He was also on board when it sailed from Belfast in 1912. Following his instructions to help with the boarding of lifeboats he led passengers to lifeboat No 5. As he steered the boat away from the *Titanic* he heard those in the water crying for help and attempted to lead the boat back to aid those people.

THE TITANIC'S CREW.

S. Freeman, a deck... What became of... is uncertain.

Mr. C. V. Clarke, one of the second-class passengers who is missing, and his wife, who is reported to have been saved.

Mr. E. N. Petty, a second-class bedroom steward. News of his fate is awaited.

the newsagency which has supplied a large pneumatic tubes lead to the departments which com—*(Daily Mirror photograph.)*

Mr. Reginald Barker, second purser, of whom nothing is yet known.

the background. The boats are about 30ft. long engers.—*(Daily Mirror photographs.)*

Mr. J. Chorley, a fireman. His friends have been torn with anxiety.

d Banfield, of Hel-...ssing. He was re-...g from a holiday.

Mr. Harry Rogers, of Tavistock, an emigrant, who is missing.

Mr. J. P. Moody, one of the mates. He is a native of Grimsby.

on board lifeboat No 2 as it left the disaster site.

Another surviving member of crew was Harold Lowe, fifth officer. He had run away to sea at the age of 14 and was on board *Titanic* prior to its departure from Belfast. Asleep during the collision itself he woke

and supported his colleagues, in particular Sixth Officer Moody, with them agreeing each to take charge of lifeboats. Lowe was put in charge of lifeboat No 14, he had fortunately taken his revolver from his cabin when he woke up and was forced to fire this during the launching of the

■ **ABOVE:** Herbert Pitman (left) and Charles Lightoller.
■ **BELOW:** Joseph Boxhall featured on ship memorabilia.

The fear though that the boat would become overfull led to Pitman steering further away.

Joseph Boxhall was the ship's fourth officer having joined the line in 1907 and was off duty when the ship struck the iceberg. He was one of the first to be sent to inspect the potential damage and after noting that the vessel was taking on water, he told Captain Smith. His importance in the sequence of events taking place was considerable; he believed that he had seen lights from another ship, which was later reported to be the SS *Californian*. Boxhall aided with the evacuation of passengers and was

■ **ABOVE & LEFT:** The *Carpathia* and its captain, A. H. Rostron.

■ **RIGHT:** Harold Lowe.

■ **BELOW:** A collapsible lifeboat, after the disaster.

■ **ABOVE:** Memorial to the engineers who died on board the *Titanic*, Southampton.

■ **ABOVE INSET:** Joseph Bell.

■ **RIGHT:** *Titanic* Musician's Memorial, Southampton.

lifeboat as more passengers tried to board the boat which was already in a dangerous position. Like Pitman he tried to return to rescue those still in the water and various attempts were made, he saved many people from certain death before his own rescue by the *Carpathia*.

Titanic's chief engineer was Joseph Bell who had had a long career with White Star Line. He was also chief engineer on board the *Olympic*. Bell was not to survive the tragedy due to his position below the water line. In all, of the 891 members of crew, 214 of them survived the disaster.

The Disaster

By noon on Wednesday 10 April 1912, the *Titanic* was ready to depart from Southampton on its maiden voyage, with 900 passengers on board. However, even the liner's departure from Southampton was not without incident as, when the massive liner gradually emerged from the dock clear from the harbour wall, the SS *New York*, which was moored close by next to the *Olympic*, was trying to break free. Thankfully the captain on board the tug was able to steer it away from danger but it seems now that it was an omen of events to come later in the voyage.

Titanic headed off to France where at Cherbourg further passengers boarded, it had arrived at the port an hour late due to the events at

■ **BELOW:** *Titanic* departs from the dock at Southampton.
■ **RIGHT:** White Star Line poster.

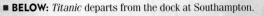

45

Southampton and at Cherbourg amongst the 274 new arrivals were some of the richer travellers including the Astors. Having left for Queenstown in Ireland the *Titanic* arrived on 11 April 1912 where a very small number of its occupants left the ship whilst 240 new passengers joined what was to become the last and longest leg of the ship's journey heading west across the Atlantic. Leaving Queenstown at 1.30pm Captain Smith had to make a decision about the course he would take to New York.

Captain Smith's decision on the route he would take for the sailing proved to be crucial. He set sail using the Autumn Southern Track which,

■ **ABOVE:** The near miss with the SS *New York*.

although was against company policy at this time of year due to the ice that ships might encounter, was made probably in order to try and post a fast sailing time. *Titanic*'s profile as the 'unsinkable' ship could've contributed to his decision with confidence in his vessel's potential performance should it run into problems. However weather conditions in that particular winter had been a lot milder than in other years and this was contributing to an increase in icebergs in the area. Despite his prophetic decision the journey progressed without any particular incidents and more than 386 miles had been traversed over the first 24 hours of sailing.

Inside the wireless room the operators knew about the potential hazardous ice conditions. Both Harold Bride and Jack Phillips had received reports about ice but they did not impede the ship's progress and the speeds *Titanic* reached saw it achieve much greater distances as it rapidly ate up the ocean in front of it.

On Sunday 14 April at 9am the *Caronia* had sent the first warning of ice fields impeding other ships in the area. Captain Smith received further notification of icebergs throughout the day but progress continued at the same rapid rate although there was acknowledgement of the presence of the icebergs in the area.

Because of the adverse weather

■ **BELOW:** *Titanic* tugged out of the dock, then for Cherbourg, France.

■ **ABOVE:** Iceberg warnings were reported in *Titanic*'s path.

■ **BELOW:** The *Titanic* drifts along a calm sea.

conditions the usual lifeboat drill which should have taken place that day did not happen – this decision was to prove fateful with many passengers unclear about what they should do or where they should go in the event of evacuation.

Unaware of the warnings, passengers continued to go about their daily activities making the most of the many facilities on board the ship which included a swimming pool and libraries filled with books. Many passengers would walk around the deck perhaps noticing the cold air but so involved with exploring the ship and its beautiful surroundings that they would have been unaware

■ **ABOVE LEFT:** Reginald Lee (top) and Fred Fleet (bottom), the *Titanic*'s look-outs on that fateful night.

■ **ABOVE:** Captain Smith.

of the potential dangers the ship was facing in the treacherous waters.

Captain Smith was attending a private party on the evening of April 14 hosted by the Widener family, returning to the bridge later that evening around 9pm. Smith discussed with his crew the weather conditions and what the status was outside of the ship. Up in the crow's nest the look-outs had taken over

their shift at 10pm. Reginald Lee and Fred Fleet were thought to be relying on their own eyesight and much was made at the inquiry over whether binoculars were made available on board the *Titanic*.

Captain Smith left the bridge at around 9.30pm leaving instructions that should any ice be seen that he was to be woken immediately. During the confusion ahead it is not

■ **ABOVE:** The crew of the *Titanic*.
■ **BELOW:** Illustration of *Titanic* approaching the iceberg.

clear that this instruction was passed down the chain of command which may have contributed to some of the disorganisation.

The chilling sight of a potential obstruction saw Fred Fleet ring the warning bell at 11.15pm to alert the bridge. He continued to try and contact the bridge by telephone and intermittently by ringing the warning bell again. Despite the repeated attempts to get hold of the crew on board the bridge, it was a while before Fleet eventually managed to speak to Moody after which there was a clear attempt to start steering the ship away from the dangerous obstruction. This delay

■ **ABOVE:** A pictorial depiction of the *Titanic* sinking.

■ **BELOW:** How the news was sent around the world.

was to be another critical moment in the chronology of the disaster; the delay in receiving the information meant that when Murdoch gave the instruction to the engineers to 'Stop: Full Speed Astern', it was far too late.

The iceberg ripped through the side of the ship causing an untold amount of damage that the crew had no idea would see the 'unsinkable' ship very quickly take on board huge amounts of sea water.

Following The Disaster

On board the *Titanic* after the impact of the vessel striking the iceberg there appeared to be no initial panic with Jack Thayer, the son of a US railway magnate, quoted as saying 'If I had a brimful glass of water in my hand not a drop would have been spilled'. Many others reported similar thoughts but in actual fact the damage caused below deck was hugely significant, the iceberg had carved a huge scar on the starboard side, which was around 12 square feet, and sea water soon began rushing through the holds of 1, 2 and 3 along with boiler room No 6.

The 'unsinkable' ship should remain afloat but with more than two of the watertight compartments being breached by water and soon flooding, it resulted in the bow of the boat starting to sink into the ocean and eventually water flooded across the bulkheads leading to more water entering the other watertight compartments. These crucial minutes were to see the crew desperately try to hinder the vast flow by trying to pump the water out of the compartments but they were working to no avail as the design that had been thought to be such a step forward in ship building was to prove fatally flawed. It is clear that the captain knew fairly early on into the disaster that the *Titanic* would not be saved.

Elsewhere on board the ship the crew were frantically trying to contact other ships within easy reach of the *Titanic*'s position. There was some doubt over the position of the ship but after the wireless room started sending out the 'SOS' distress code the plight of the *Titanic* was to be witnessed by the RMS *Carpathia* which immediately sailed towards the direction of the stricken ship where itself was in danger of coming into contact with icebergs and putting itself and its crew at risk. That terrible night was to see the *Carpathia* and its crew aid many of those who had managed to escape *Titanic* via the lifeboats.

Time was starting to slip by quickly on board the *Titanic* with options running out for Captain Smith and his crew. The lifeboats were uncovered by crewmembers shortly after midnight with the order to prioritise women and children whilst boarding them. Throughout this period there were still ongoing attempts to try and ease the situation below decks but the pressure was rising rapidly in the boiler room.

Flares were fired at 12.45am just at the same time as lifeboat No 7 was departing the ship. The earlier decision to not hold the morning lifeboat drill had horrendous consequences. There was a general lack of organisation with key personnel not clear on what they should be doing or where, and missing

■ **RIGHT:** Captain Rostron (seated centre) and officers of the SS *Carpathia*.

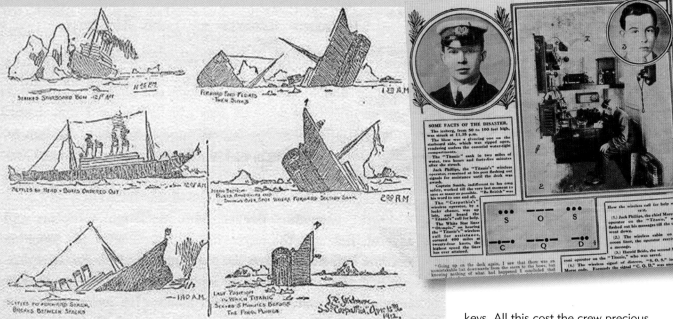

SKETCHES OF THE TITANIC BY "JACK" THAYER

These sketches were outlined by John B. Thayer, Jr., on the day of the disaster, and afterwards filled in by L. D. Skidmon, of Brooklyn.

■ **ABOVE:** An illustration drawn by Jack Thayer after the disaster.
■ **ABOVE RIGHT:** *Titanic* distress calls.
■ **BELOW:** *Titanic* rescue memorabilia stamps.

keys. All this cost the crew precious time and at a terrible price with passengers losing their lives due to this lack of clarity.

As has been well reported, many of the lifeboats were not full to capacity, some lifeboats had only 25 people on them and others contained men who were close by the lifeboats as they were ready to depart rather than waiting for further women and children to board – other passengers leapt into lifeboats as they were being lowered into the ocean, they were willing to risk their lives rather than stay on board a ship that by now they had realised was definitely going to sink.

On lifeboat No 1 only 12 people were boarded including Sir Cosmo Duff-Gordon and his party along with seven members of crew. It was inconceivable to think that 40 people should have been on that lifeboat and only 12 left the sinking vessel on it. Most other lifeboats had a capacity of 65 but in the case of No 8 only 28 passengers and crew were on board, similar numbers were on board other lifeboats and clearly tensions were extremely high with crew rushing to lower the lifeboats before they were full to capacity – terrified that they would not escape with their lives if they were to stay and collect more passengers.

Whilst understandable this left many unable to board other lifeboats, leaving them to die or to try and swim to lifeboats when they fell from the ship as it was sinking. So many stories of tragedy, heroism and bravery took place that night. Panic spread as some of these stories reached other lifeboats, invoking terror as those left tried to rush lifeboats causing crew in charge having to launch the remaining lifeboats to prevent them from becoming overloaded with passengers. The entry into the sea was not without danger as the lack of practice could have seen some lifeboats hitting others as they were lowered too quickly.

In the wireless room the operators had been working tirelessly sending

■ **RIGHT, BELOW & BOTTOM:** Lifeboats being frantically lowered but sparsely filled.

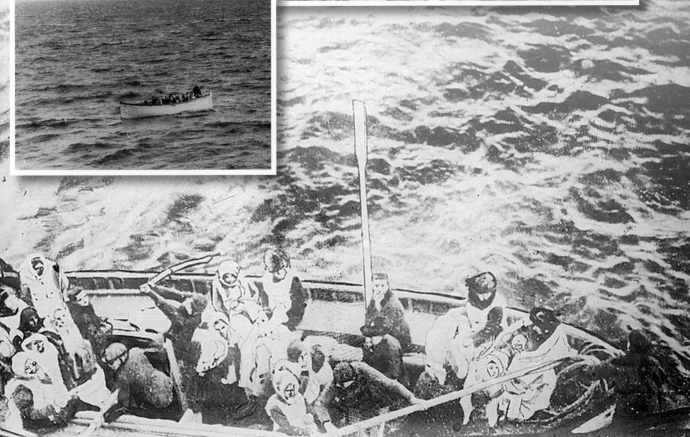

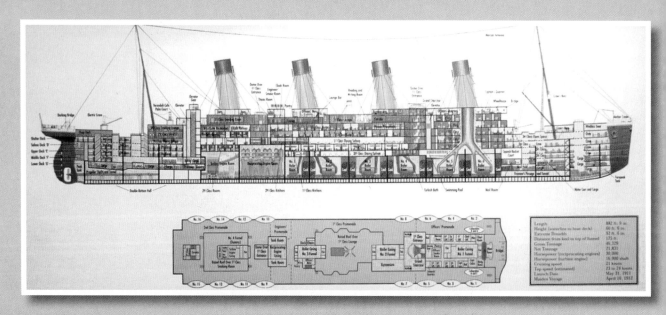

■ **ABOVE:** *Titanic* finally sinks at 2.20am.
■ **OPPOSITE LEFT ABOVE:** Plan of the *Titanic*, showing lifeboat layout.
■ **OPPOSITE LEFT:** The last few minutes, before the ship sank.

distress signals to garner further help for the stricken liner however, it was clear now that failing power and the increase of water on board the ship meant that their task was coming to a rapid end; Captain Smith arrived at around 2am and relieved Bride and Phillips of their duties.

By 2am there were varying scenes of chaos as passengers and crew, now clearly aware that the ship was likely to sink, tried to make their escape. With over 1,500 passengers and crew still on board the *Titanic* others, like the band that played on, took refuge in other activities –

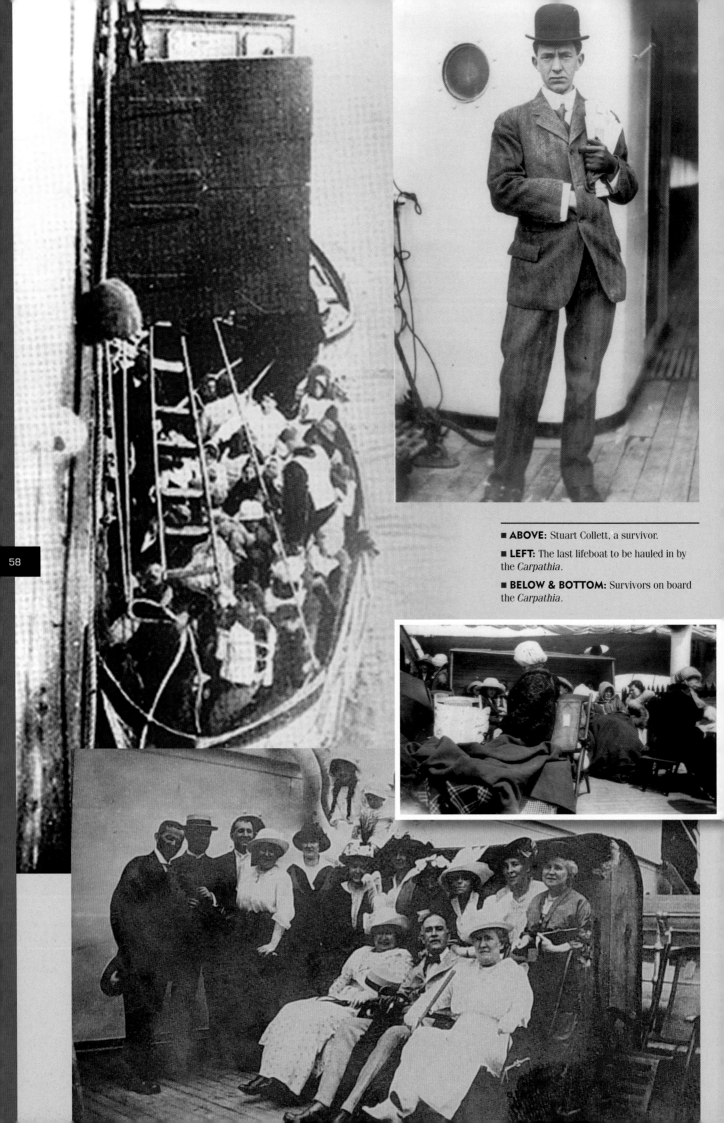

58

■ **ABOVE:** Stuart Collett, a survivor.

■ **LEFT:** The last lifeboat to be hauled in by the *Carpathia*.

■ **BELOW & BOTTOM:** Survivors on board the *Carpathia*.

some even played cards seemingly oblivious to their eventual fate.

As the ship listed, explosions that could now be heard within the ship as boilers and other vital equipment began to overload, horrified further people. At around 2.15am the ship's lighting gave out and by now the *Titanic* gave itself up to the dark waters with it starting to disappear underneath the ocean at around 2.20am.

Those who had made it into lifeboats now had to wait for rescue, uncertain as to whether any ship would make it to them. Finally at 2.45am the *Carpathia* reached the ice field carving its way carefully through the dangerous waters in order to try and rescue survivors whilst trying to ensure its own safety. Rockets from *Carpathia* were spotted by those in lifeboats and around 4am it reached the area where the *Titanic* was last thought to have been. However as the wireless operators had wrongly given out the initial location, no one was seen. A short time later crew on board the *Carpathia* spotted a distress flare and over the next few hours it aided

with boarding those in lifeboats to safety. The *Californian* arrived at around 8.50am and aided with the search, which was abandoned after

■ **ABOVE:** Lowering the *Titanic's* lifeboats from the *Carpathia* after she docked in New York.

■ **RIGHT INSET:** Lord Mersey, chair of the British inquiry and William Alden Smith (below).

■ **BELOW:** Waiting for news of survivors in Southampton.

- **LEFT:** Survivors on their way home.
- **BELOW:** Rescued crew in New York, USA.
- **BOTTOM LEFT:** Wireless operator Harold Bride arrives in London.
- **BOTTOM RIGHT:** Archie Jewell, one of the look-outs giving evidence.

10.30 when no further survivors or wreckage was found.

Approximately 705 passengers and crew were rescued by the *Carpathia* and *Californian* with around 1,523 fatalities although these numbers are uncertain. Following the disaster White Star Line sent four ships to the location where the disaster had happened to try and pick up bodies. Around 328 bodies were found with a large number of these buried at sea and a small number being buried in cemeteries in Halifax, Nova Scotia.

With such a loss of life there was the desire to find out why the disaster had happened and inquiries were held both in New York and in London after crew and survivors had returned to Britain. Lord Mersey was scathing in his report about

the SS *Californian*'s failure to make efforts to reach the boat. There was a conclusion drawn that the great speed that the *Titanic* was travelling at plus the decision to travel through treacherous ice fields was a large factor in the terrible tragedy.

The after effects of the *Titanic*'s loss were felt widely with many new safety features being introduced on board other ships and regulations around speed when in the vicinity of ice fields.

The key finding though, was that in future ships needed to carry enough lifeboats to fit all passengers and crew on in the event of such a disaster. Its sister ships, *Olympic* and *Britannic*, were modified to this effect. It is true that because of the demise of *Titanic* other ships were to become safer but the huge loss of life is a terrible price to pay for others' safety. As we approach the 100th anniversary of the loss of the *Titanic* there will be many events dedicated to remembering the liner and those passengers who lost their lives. A cruise taking the original route that the *Titanic* followed is due to take place in April 2012 with the same number of passengers on board as was on the *Titanic*. A memorial is due to take place on board in the place where the ship hit the iceberg. Cities closely associated with the ship will also remember the loss with various events taking place including musicals and memorial dinners.

■ **ABOVE:** Sir Cosmo Duff-Gordon giving his evidence at the inquiry.

■ **BELOW:** Bruce Ismay gives his turn of events.

Remembering the *Titanic*

■ **BELOW:** Actor Kenneth More shakes hands with Mr S. E. Daniels, a survivor of the *Titanic*, at the premiere of *A Night to Remember*.

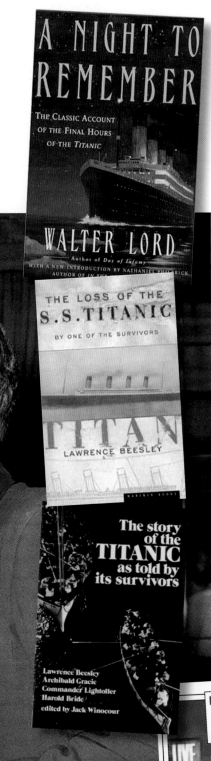

With events taking place to remember the loss of the *Titanic* throughout the months preceding its 100th anniversary there will be a vast array of merchandise produced, including numerous books. However those early books that were published by survivors provide a chilling insight into the events on board the ship itself.

The first books to appear were those compiled by Lawrence Beesley – *The Loss of the SS Titanic* – and by Archibald Gracie – *The Truth about the Titanic*. The photographic archive compiled by Father Browne has been widely published in books, whilst the Ulster Folk and Transport Museum at Cultra now houses a significant photographic archive, much of it drawn from the Harland & Wolff Collection.

Inevitably there are societies and websites devoted to the *Titanic* and its sister ships. Apart from the wide-ranging content offered by Wikipedia, there are sites like titanic-facts.com, titanichistoricalsociety.org, encyclopedia-titanica.org, titanicinternationalsociety.org, titanicheritagetrust.org.uk and titanic-titanic.com. These sites offer a wide range of historical material and documentary evidence relating to White Star Line and the three 'Olympic' class liners. The continuing interest in the company and its ill-fated ships is demonstrated by the sheer range of books and other items available from the online shops featured by many of the sites. The new media of social networking will also be 'trending' around the 100th anniversary events. With Facebook groups on the subject already set up modern communication methods will also serve to keep the memories alive.

With a story as dramatic as the *Titanic*, it was inevitable that a number of feature films would be made about the sinking. The first, released shortly after the actual sinking, in May 1912, was a silent movie that starred Dorothy Gibson entitled *Saved from the Titanic*. Gibson had been a passenger on the ill-fated voyage and had escaped on lifeboat No 7. The disappearance of the print marks a huge loss in the ephemera associated with *Titanic*.

A film in 1958, based on the book *A Night to Remember* with a screenplay by Eric Ambler, was released two years after the book. Directed by Roy Baker

■ **LEFT:** Books published about the *Titanic*.

■ **BELOW:** Relics rescued from the *Titanic*.

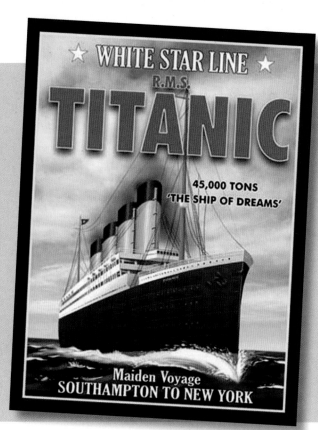

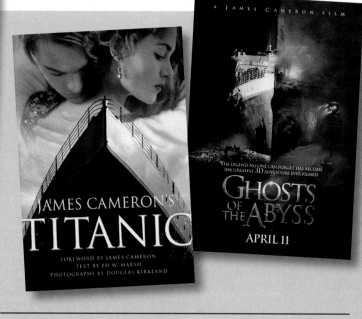

■ **ABOVE:** James Cameron blockbusters.

■ **LEFT:** White Star Line maiden voyage poster.

– whose background in documentary filmmaking during the war gave many of his films an authentic feel – and starring such luminaries as Honor Blackman, David McCallum and Kenneth More, the film was shot at Pinewood Studios with the nearby Ruislip Lido used to replicate the North Atlantic.

Of all the films inspired by the tragedy, Lew Grade's *Raise the Titanic!* was perhaps the most far-fetched. Released in 1980 and based upon a novel by Clive Cussler, the storyline revolved around the presence on board the wreck of a highly prized mineral – 'byzanium' – that was essential for a secret defence project. Much derided by the press at the time the scene of the *Titanic* being raised from the ocean is nonetheless chilling.

More recently, the highly successful director James Cameron has produced narrative and documentary films on the *Titanic*. Until the recent release of the same director's *Avatar*, *Titanic*, starring Leonardo DiCaprio and Kate Winslet, released in 1997, was the highest grossing film in history. The ambition of the film and its commercial success was also reflected in its critical triumph in winning no fewer than 11 Academy Awards, including Best Picture and Best Director, in 1998. In 2003, Cameron followed this success with, *Ghosts of the Abyss*, which used two cameras to gain access to the wreck itself and film the interior of the liner. It used CGI technology to recreate how the ship would have looked 100 years ago when it was first launched – a fitting memorial. Cameron's *Titanic* is currently being converted to 3D and will have a spring 2012 release date to coincide with the 100th anniversary.

■ **ABOVE:** Lew Grade and (inset) *Raise the Titanic*.

■ **LEFT:** SS *Nomadic*, originally a tender of the White Star Line *Olympic* and *Titanic* ships.